THRILL
SEEKERS

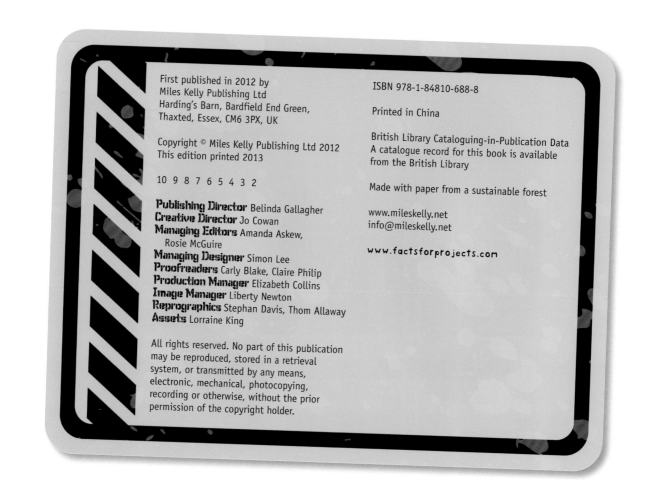

First published in 2012 by
Miles Kelly Publishing Ltd
Harding's Barn, Bardfield End Green,
Thaxted, Essex, CM6 3PX, UK

Copyright © Miles Kelly Publishing Ltd 2012
This edition printed 2013

10 9 8 7 6 5 4 3 2

Publishing Director Belinda Gallagher
Creative Director Jo Cowan
Managing Editors Amanda Askew,
    Rosie McGuire
Managing Designer Simon Lee
Proofreaders Carly Blake, Claire Philip
Production Manager Elizabeth Collins
Image Manager Liberty Newton
Reprographics Stephan Davis, Thom Allaway
Assets Lorraine King

ISBN 978-1-84810-688-8

Printed in China

British Library Cataloguing-in-Publication Data
A catalogue record for this book is available
from the British Library

Made with paper from a sustainable forest

www.mileskelly.net
info@mileskelly.net

www.factsforprojects.com

ACKNOWLEDGMENTS

The publishers would like to thank the following sources for the use
of their photographs:

KEY t=top, b=bottom, c=center, l=left, r=right
AL=Alamy, B=Bridgeman, CO=Corbis, F=Fotolia, FLPA=Frank Lane Picture
Agency, GI=Getty Images, IS=istockphoto.com, NPL=Nature Picture Library,
PL=Photolibrary, RF=Rex Features, SPL=Science Photo Library,
S=Shutterstock, TF=Topfoto

COVER Franck Seguin/CO **BACK COVER** Brooke Whatnall/S
1 taboga/S; **2** Pedro Nogueira/S; **3**(bg) Werner Muenzker/S, (strip, left to
right) Deymos/S, Dainis Derics/S, A Cotton Photo/S, Vasco Oliveira/S, Vitalii
Nesterchuk/S; **4–5** Unimedia Images/RF; **6–7** Werner Muenzker/RF; **6** GI,
(br) Daniel Ramsbott/dpa/CO; **7**(br) Roger-Viollet/RF, (c) Unimedia
Images/RF, (t) Deymos/S; **8–9** Thomas Zobl/S; **8**(b) Kesu/S, (bl) GI;
9(br) Petrosg, (c) Sam Tinson/RF, (c) Cre8tive Images/S, (tl) Ulza/S,
(tr) Christopher Groenhout/GI; **10** Wronaavd/S, (r) Kokhanchikov/S,
(cr) Martin Lehmann/S, (tc) Martin Lehmann/S, (tl) Martin Lehmann/S;
11(c) fuyu liu/S, (bl) GI, (br) National Geographic Image Collection/AL,
(t) Sports Illustrated/GI; **12–13** Nicemonkey/S; **12**(bl) National
Geographic/Everett/RF, (br) Marcel Jancovic/S, (t) A Cotton Photo/S;
13(b) Hugh Sitton/CO, (t) Amy Toensing/GI, (tl) Alfredo Dagli Orti/The Art
Archive/CO; **14–15** maga/S; **14**(tr) Tyler Stableford/GI, (t) GI;
15(bc) ullsteinbild/TF, (bl) Jakub Krechowicz/S, (br) Morphart/S, (tl) Vitaly
Korovin/S, (tl) The Granger Collection/TF, (tr) GI; **16–17** Losevsky Pavel/S,
(c) Steve Maisey/RF; **16**(bl) Hulton-Deutsch Collection/CO, (bl) Christophe
Boisson/S, (cl) Lightspring/S, (tl) bepsy/S, (tl) Christophe Boisson/S,
(tr) Perov Stanislav/S; **17**(br) Bongarts/GI, (t) AFP/GI; **18–19** Mikhail
Nekrasov/S, NitroCephal/S, (b) Nino Cavalier/S, (b) Kellis/S; **18**(bl) Mariana
Bazo/X00023/Reuters/CO, (bl) Sergey Mironov/S, (br/tr) Chayne Hultgren
(www.thespacecowboy.com), (c) Ton Lammerts/S; **19**(br) Sipa Press/RF,
(tc) DJTaylor/S, (tl) KeystoneUSA-ZUMA/RF, (tr) Kacso Sandor/S; **20**(b) Jack
Dempsey/AP/PAI, (b) ajt/S, (tr) Alfredo Escobar/epa/CO; **21**(c) Nils Z/S,
(b) John D McHugh/AFP/GI, (cl) Alexis Rosenfeld/SPL, (t) Bettmann/CO;
22–23(tc) Steve Marcus/Reuters/CO; **22**(b) William West/AFP/GI,
(b) saiko3p/S; **23**(b) Paul Roberts/Offside/CO, (bc) patrimonio designs
limited/S, (t) GI, (tc) Ian O'Hanlon/S; **24–25** National Geographic/GI,
swinner/S, (b) Mark S. Cosslett/GI; **24** Fedorov Oleksiy/S, (t) National
Geographic/GI; **25**(b) Barcroft Media/GI, (t) Stephen Alvarez/GI;
26(br) Benoit Stichelbaut/bluegreenpictures.com/RF, (c) Mary Evans Picture
Library/AL, (tl) marekuliasz/S; **27**(br) Charles Platiau/Reuters/CO, (tl) RF,
(tr) Sipa Press/RF; **28–29** Action Press/RF; **28**(bl) Gamma-Rapho/GI;
29(r) WireImage/GI, (r) Maria Toutoudaki/IS, (bl) Rick Doyle/CO,
(tl) Agencia EFE/RF, (tl) Anan Kaewkhammul/S; **30–31**(b) Maygutyak/F;
30 Tim Clayton/CO, (b) Peter Klaunzer/epa/CO, (tl) shutswis/S;
31(cr) MountainHardcore/S, (r) Aurora Photos/AL, (t) Ross Woodhall/GI,
(tl) Walter Quirtmair/S; **32–33** Rob Howarth/RF; **32**(cl) Bettmann/CO;
33(br) Tyler Stableford/GI, (tl) Swim Ink 2, LLC/CO, (tr) GI Sport;
34–35 Sam Cornwell/S, (c) taboga/S, (t) Claudio Santana/AFP/GI,
(tc) Creatista/S; **34**(bl) Brooke Whatnall/S, (l) DGDesign/S, (l) Poprugin
Aleksey/S; **35**(bl) 808isgreat/S, (br) GI, (r) Arne Dedert/epa/CO;
36–37 Ljupco Smokovski/S, benchart/S, Christophe Boisson/S;
36(br) William West/AFP/GI, (c) Popperfoto/GI, (tr) Ken McKay/RF;
37(br) GI, (tr) Starstock/PS; **38–39** charles taylor/S, Dr. Morley Read/S;
38(r) F, (bc) c.IFC Films/Everett/RF, (br) Taiga/S, (l) c.IFC Films/Everett/RF,
(tr) airn/S; **39**(bl) migin/IS, (bl) Gemenacom/S, (br) f9photos/S,
(br) Michael C. Gray/S, (cr) Face to Face/PS, (cr) FoxSearch/Everett/RF,
(tl) AP/PAI, (tr) GI

All other photographs are from: Corel, digitalSTOCK, digitalvision,
Dreamstime.com, Fotolia.com, iStockphoto.com, John Foxx, PhotoAlto,
PhotoDisc, PhotoEssentials, PhotoPro, Stockbyte

Every effort has been made to acknowledge the source and copyright
holder of each picture. The publishers apologise for any unintentional
errors or omissions.

THRILL
SEEKERS

Richard Platt

Consultant: Philip Steele

Miles Kelly

CONTENTS

◀ Swiss pilot Yves Rossy is the first person to fly for a
set period of time using a wingsuit. In 2011, he flew
across the Grand Canyon, Arizona, U.S.

Taking to THE SKIES

Dropping like a stone from a high-flying aircraft would be a white-knuckle, breathtaking dare for most of us. But for some thrill seekers, ordinary skydiving is just far too dull. Instead, they push risk to the limit, jumping fast and low, from earthbound objects, or in tight formation.

BASE JUMPING IS THE WORLD'S MOST DANGEROUS SPORT, WITH ONE IN EVERY 60 JUMPS ENDING IN DEATH. SURVIVAL IS UNLIKELY ON BASE JUMPS LOWER THAN ABOUT 200 FT (60 M).

Back to base

Why bother with an aircraft, when there's plenty of tall stuff on the ground from which to launch yourself? Base jumping gets its name from the things you can climb to start your plunge—Buildings, Antennas, Spans (bridges), and Earth (cliffs). Base jumpers may be falling for only 10–15 seconds— barely enough time for an ordinary parachute to open. So they jump with special equipment that opens fast and reliably. Despite these precautions, a slight misjudgment can mean a deadly fall.

▲ Spanning a canyon, with a long clear drop below, this road bridge makes an ideal launch point for a base jumper, though he risks arrest if he's caught.

Patterns in the clouds

Formation freefall skydivers aim to link hands and descend in a regular pattern, with each person steering themselves into a prearranged place. Collisions are the biggest danger because they can knock a jumper unconscious, leaving them unable to open their parachute. To combat this, many wear an automatic deployment device that opens their reserve chute at a preset altitude if they don't pull the rip cord.

▶ This 36-way diamond formation drop over Eisenach, Germany, would be perfect… if only those two people at the top had grabbed their buddies' legs!

Below the radar

Special Forces parachutists drop from 25,000 ft (7,600 m). HALO (High-Altitude, Low-Opening) drops offer the least chance of detection, because the soldiers freefall to the lowest safe altitude before opening their parachutes. In HAHO (High-Altitude, High-Opening) drops, their aircraft need not fly over enemy territory. The troops deploy their square, mattress-like chutes quickly, and use them to glide for up to an hour, landing up to 25 mi (40 km) behind enemy lines.

◀ Special Forces jump from such high altitudes that they must breathe bottled oxygen because the air is so thin.

▲ Swiss "Jetman" Yves Rossy has taken wingsuits a huge step further by fitting four engines to a rigid wing. Strapped to his back, it carried him across the English Channel in 2008 at 186 mph (299 km/h).

Soaring on air

Like bats or flying foxes, wingsuit skydivers steer their descent using fabric flaps under their arms and between their legs. These "wings" allow them to fly horizontally, usually zooming 2.5 ft (70 cm) forward for each foot (30 cm) they fall—a glide ratio of 2.5. Wingpacks, made of rigid carbon fiber, can increase the glide ratio to 6. Base jumpers have begun using wingsuits, prolonging their falls from seconds into minutes.

GERMAN BATMAN

Wingpacks are less than 20 years old, but German engineer Otto Lilienthal (1848–1896) pioneered a gliding wing in 1890. He had the bad luck to live in one of the flattest areas of Europe—the North German Plain—so he built an artificial hill from which to fly his batlike craft. Leaping from his *Fliegeberg* (flight-hill) in 1896, Lilienthal rose to 56 ft (17 m), before crashing and breaking his spine. His dying words were "Small sacrifices must be made."

Otto Lilienthal's first gliding trials with his fragile wing took him just a little way off the ground. The more ambitious flights that followed inspired American brothers Orville and Wilbur Wright, who in 1903 built the world's first aircraft.

Playing with FIRE

For once, your parents were right! Playing with fire really is dangerous, so don't try any of these tricks at home. Performers who eat, breathe, and dance with fire have learned their searing skills from experts. They risk painful burns each time they kindle the flames that light up their superhot acts.

▼ Expert fire-eaters put torches right into their mouths, closing their lips to put out the flames.

BREATHING FLAMES

It's not just fearsome legendary beasts that breathe fire. Circus performers spout flames so hot that they need special insurance in case they ignite the audience. To impersonate a dragon, they first take mouthfuls of fuel. Then, taking care to stand with their backs to the wind, they blow across lighted torches, creating spectacular bursts of flame. Burns are the obvious danger, but there are plenty more—swallowing or inhaling fuel can put performers in hospital.

A VERY HOT MEAL

Even the hottest of curries can't rival a feast of fire. Fire-eaters dine on real flames flashing from tapers and torches. How do they do it? There's no trickery involved, and there's no such thing as a "cold flame." It's the fire-eaters' saliva that protects them. By licking their lips and keeping their mouths moist, they create a cooling barrier against the flame's heat.

▼ On a darkened stage, flames trace the movements of this Samoan knife fire-dancer.

FANS OF FLAMES

To the Samoans who dance it, *ailao afi* is a modern take on a knife-whirling warrior tradition. To the watching crowd, it's a breathtaking performance of spinning flames and sharp blades. Fire-dancing traditions in Samoa and elsewhere have inspired gymnasts and jugglers to add flaming chains, poles, and hoops to their own acts.

▶ Firewalking is one of a number of rituals that take place during the Jia Chai festival in Phuket, Thailand.

▲ The pillar of flame from a fire-breather's mouth may burn hotter than 2,000°F (1,100°C).

FIRE-BREATHER ANTONIO RESTIVO BLEW THE WORLD'S BIGGEST FLAME IN JANUARY 2011. AT 26.5 FT (8.05 M), IT WAS AS LONG AS A BUS.

BAREFOOT ORDEAL

In a ceremony that's 3,000 years old, religious people pray for help and protection—then test their faith by walking barefoot on glowing embers! In fact, this "ordeal" is not proof of divine protection. Though the coals may be at 1,700°F (930°C), ashes don't conduct heat well. As long as walkers keep moving, the thick skin on their soles protects their feet. This doesn't mean firewalking is safe—walkers suffer agonizing burns if they trip, or if the coals are ill-prepared.

Death-defying DIVES

For cliff divers, hitting the water is the end of the thrill, but for breath-hold and ice divers it is just the beginning. However for participants in every form of diving sport, water is a potentially lethal hazard—capable of breaking limbs and sucking air from the lungs.

Daring plunge

What began in 1935 as a tourist-pleasing stunt in Acapulco, Mexico, is now a popular extreme sport. It is the height of the dives that makes cliff-diving extreme. Typically 85 ft (26 m) from the water, the rocky jumping-off points are 2.5 times higher than an Olympic board. Divers plunge at 50–60 mph (85–100 km/h), and to avoid injury they adopt a torpedo-like pose when they enter the water.

▼ In the spectacular drop to the water at Switzerland's narrow Ponte Brolla gorge, Swiss diver Andy Hulliger performed a double back somersault with two twists. This dive—and others—won him fourth place in the 2011 European Cliff Diving Championship.

EVEN FOR PROFESSIONALS, CLIFF DIVING IS RISKY, AND EACH YEAR AMATEUR IMITATORS ARE KILLED OR CRIPPLED.

MANY FREEDIVERS USE YOGA OR MEDITATION BEFORE A DIVE TO SLOW THEIR METABOLISM AND REDUCE THEIR OXYGEN NEEDS.

1 ft Your eardrums flex inward and you feel pressure in your ears

6 ft Water pressure starts to tear the tissue of your eardrums if you lack training

10 ft Pressure on the lungs makes it impossible to suck air down a tube from the surface

20 ft Lung squeeze reverses natural buoyancy, causing you to sink

60 ft Lungs compressed to one quarter of the surface size

Into the deep

How long can you hold your breath? Sixty seconds is pretty good, but the best freedivers can manage eight or nine minutes! Freedivers compete to swim as deep as 870 ft (265 m) without breathing apparatus. In competitions their descents are divided into many categories with different rules. The scariest is No-Limits Apnea, in which the freediver grips a weighted sled to sink like a stone. When they can go no deeper, an air-filled bag brings them to the surface.

▼ The ocean's depths hold no fear for British/Caymanian freediver Tanya Streeter. She holds the women's world record for No-Limits Apnea, with a descent to 525 ft (160 m).

BENEATH THE ANTARCTIC

Scientists working in Antarctica dive in temperatures below 32°F (0°C) to study life in the shallow coastal water around the southern continent. Getting into the water isn't easy—they must first use giant augers (drilling tools) to bore holes in the 6-ft-(1.8-m-) thick ice. The water beneath is among the world's clearest, and divers combat its low temperature with dry suits and layered underwear. Getting out can be as hard as getting in—divers must share their ice-holes with fat Weddell seals surfacing to breathe.

▼ Returning to the hole in the ice is vital, so it's marked with a weighted safety line, flags, and flashing lights that divers can see from a great distance away.

PEARL DIVERS BRING ONE TON OF OYSTERS TO THE WATER'S SURFACE TO FIND JUST THREE OR FOUR PEARLS IN THEIR SHELLS.

▼ This breath-hold diver heads for the surface with a net full of black pearl oysters at Fakarava Atoll in French Polynesia. Today's divers don't rely on luck and chance—pearls are farmed here.

Seabed harvest

Breath-hold diving has a long history—3,000 years ago in ancient Greece, salvage divers were given bonuses according to how deep they could swim to retrieve the precious cargoes of sunken galleys. In the centuries that followed, divers held their breath to pluck sponges, pearls, shellfish, and even pirate treasure from the seabed. The invention of scuba (Self-Contained Underwater Breathing Apparatus) in the mid-20th century made these risky diving feats unnecessary.

BEASTLY Beasts

◀ This scuba-diving cameraman is taking a grave risk. Tiger sharks are second only to great whites in their record for attacks on humans.

People have lived, worked, and played with wild animals for more than 30,000 years. For most of this time, the beasts got a raw deal, mostly as entertainment for humans. Now that animals in the wild are vanishing fast, we take better care of our savage friends—but interaction with potentially lethal creatures demands extreme caution.

Making friends with Jaws

Long persecuted as killers, sharks are now getting the scientific attention they deserve. They need it—numbers are falling and up to half of all shark species are endangered. Of some 380 shark species, just four are known to attack humans. Scientists study these cautiously. Armored suits protect against a friendly nibble, but when Jaws is big—and hungry—only a cage will do.

Pooch or pack?

British wolf researcher Shaun Ellis has an unconventional approach to studying wolves. To learn about these notorious and misunderstood wild dogs he joined—and led—a wolf pack in Idaho, U.S., learning to live, hunt, eat, and howl just like them. Today he uses his knowledge to help wolves and humans live in harmony in areas where packs' territories are close to people's homes.

◀ At his refuge in Devon, U.K., Shaun Ellis combines research with a TV program to educate the public about wolves and their behavior.

▲ Handlers carry "weapons," but do not hurt the dogs they train.

He's only playing!

In the cruel and illegal "sport" of dogfighting, owners *try* to make their dogs aggressive, but not all attack dogs are savage. The police and the military use dogs for law enforcement and security. Living suspects are more useful than dead ones, so handlers train their canine colleagues to chase and hold onto fleeing villains, slowing them down until an officer arrives. It shouldn't hurt, but trainers wear padded clothes, just in case.

Spots or stripes?

Studying large predators in the wild is a risky business, and scientists have to take care to avoid being confused with their subjects' natural prey. They use box traps and tranquilizer darts to make animals safe to handle, then often tag them for radio tracking. Even a tagged animal can be a danger—the tracking receiver shows only direction, not distance, and isn't accurate when the tagged animal is very nearby.

▲ Scientists in Colorado, U.S., release a captured lynx into its natural environment after fitting it with a radio collar to track its movements.

KAZAKHSTAN FALCONERS RAISE BIRDS FROM CHICKS, RISKING THEIR LIVES TO TAKE THEM FROM NESTS ON REMOTE CRAGS.

▼ Thick gloves protect a Kazakhstani falconer's outstretched arms from the sharp talons of his beloved eagle.

Swooping hunters

In medieval Europe, falconry was considered the noblest of the hunting arts. The more noble the nobleman, the bigger the bird that perched on his gloved fist. This must make today's Kazakhstan hunters the royalty of falconers, for they hunt with the world's biggest raptors—golden eagles. These powerful birds weigh as much as a small turkey, and have a 7 ft (2 m) wingspan.

SERIOUS Summits

Watch a skilled climber scale a rock wall, and you'll realize why this demanding sport has been nicknamed the "vertical dance." The elegant, graceful movements of top mountaineers are not just for show. They conserve energy, keep the climbers balanced, and—most importantly—protect them from potentially fatal falls.

Defying gravity

Clinging by your fingertips from vertical rock may look risky, but expert climbers fix their safety ropes to anchors (metal devices wedged in the rock) at regular intervals. Although this technique (known as "lead climbing") reduces risk, a leader who slips will fall the distance to their latest starting point, plus the slack of the rope. However, even on popular and dizzyingly high rock faces, fatal accidents are rare, because experienced climbers tutor novices in safety and caution.

◄ "Soloing" (climbing without the protection of a safety rope) on a route such as El Cap in Yosemite Park, U.S., is highly dangerous—a single error could lead to a fatal fall.

IN THE "DEATH ZONE," ABOVE 26,000 FT (8,000 M), THE AIR IS SO THIN THAT NO CLIMBER CAN SURVIVE FOR LONG.

◄ To get up ice walls like this cave in Iceland's Langjökull glacier, climbers use hollow ice screws. They turn them securely into the ice, then fix safety ropes through rings at the ends.

Super-slippery slope

Ice is as slippy as rock is grippy, so winter climbing requires different techniques. Even on quite gentle slopes an ice climber needs crampons—sharp spikes fixed to boot soles. To get up really steep slopes such as frozen waterfalls, climbers swing special pointed axes into the ice, looping safety ropes through protection (anchors) screwed into the frozen surface.

"Because it's there"

The world's great peaks are often in remote locations. Reaching them means days of walking, carrying everything you need for the whole trip. The atmosphere gets thinner the higher you go, forcing climbers to gulp oxygen from gas bottles. So why climb a high mountain? English climber George Mallory famously answered "because it's there" before climbing the world's highest peak, Everest.

▶ Mallory (shown here in the Alps) probably reached Everest's summit in 1924, but he and his partner Sandy Irvine died while descending the mountain.

High, light, and fast

Italian climber Reinhold Messner leads the world in Alpinism—the art of climbing fast, high, and with few supplies and equipment. In May 1978, he and fellow climber Peter Habeler climbed Everest without bottled oxygen, a feat previously considered impossible. Two years later Messner did it again—alone!

▲ The greatest climber of all time, Messner was the first to ascend all the world's peaks higher than 26,000 ft (8,000 m). Here he points to Everest soon after his lone ascent.

Pioneer of the peaks

The thin air of high mountains causes altitude sickness. Those affected suffer blinding headaches, exhaustion, dizziness, and confusion. German explorer and mountaineer Alexander von Humboldt was the first to describe it, after climbing Ecuador's Chimborazo volcano in 1802. This wasn't the only hardship he suffered in South America. He dodged vampire bats, cannibals, alligators, and a club-waving madman!

▶ German explorer and naturalist Alexander von Humboldt (1769–1859) gave his name to a dozen places and almost as many natural features.

Symptoms of altitude sickness

1. Headaches (may even appear at the altitude of a ski resort).

2. Climbing higher causes dizziness, tiredness, and breathlessness.

3. Hands and feet swell and the nose bleeds.

4. In severe altitude sickness, sufferers get a dry cough they can't shake. Headaches worsen and nausea begins.

5. Extreme altitude eventually kills climbers—fluid collects in their tissues, causing the brain to swell.

High-flying THRILLS

Soaring, spinning, leaping, and balancing high above the ring, circus acrobats risk deadly falls twice daily to entertain big-top audiences. Safety nets or harnesses can break a fall, but do not completely remove the danger, and the most daring aerial artists perform without protection at alarming heights.

▶ These two young performers from the Chinese State Circus are using parasols to help keep their balance on the high wire.

▶ Gymnasts performing on silks use thick fabric, which is at least 5 ft (1.5 m) wide.

Ropes and silks

Though more gymnastic than acrobatic, free-hanging rope or ribbon acts expose the performer to dangerous, unbroken falls. Mastery of these acts involves learning to climb from the ground, gripping and balancing on the rope or ribbon without using the hands, and—most demanding of all—releasing it to drop suddenly down in a controlled spin. Performers use rosin (pine resin) to increase their grip.

HIGH HISTORY

Legendary French acrobat Charles Blondin set a standard for rope-walking that has never been equaled. His most famous feat, performed in 1859, was to cross America's Niagara Falls on a 1,100-ft- (335-m-) long rope. Simply walking across was too simple for Blondin—he also did it blindfolded, pushing a wheelbarrow, on stilts, and carrying his manager on his back. He even stopped in the middle to cook and eat an omelet.

◀ Stretched tight 160 ft (almost 50 m) above the churning waterfall, Blondin's rope was the width of a person's forearm.

Big-top balance

Invented in China, rope-walking is the most ancient form of altitude acrobatics. It was popular in ancient Rome—2nd-century emperor Marcus Aurelius passed a law that forced rope-walkers to use a safety net. Today, a steel wire has replaced the traditional rope, and stabilizer cables stop it swaying on long spans. Walkers also use a bar to help them balance and to walk in winds that would otherwise be dangerous.

At the Winter Circus in Paris in 2009, members of the Bouglione troop entertain on the same spot where Jules Leotard performed the very first trapeze show 150 years earlier.

TRAPEZE ARTISTS HURTLE THROUGH THE AIR AT SPEEDS OF MORE THAN 60 MPH (100 KM/H).

Playing catch

The most gripping aerial act is the flying trapeze, in which performers hurl and catch each other high above the crowd. The flyer must be nimble and light, the catcher must be strong, and timing is vital for all involved. Almost all trapeze artists perform above nets, but an awkward fall to the net may cause serious injury.

Cable-car lines are ready-made for high-wire acts. In 2009 Swiss wire-walker Freddy Nock climbed one to the top of the Zugspitze, Germany's highest peak.

Taking it outside

Outdoor high-wire acts require special preparation. The team rigging the wire must be sure that the anchor points at each end are strong enough to take the enormous tension in the wire without breaking. Wires have additional diagonal cables to stop them swaying in the wind. Even with these precautions performers are at considerable risk—and must even check the weather forecast for lightning warnings.

BLADES and POINTS

In a crowded street, a half-naked performer chops a cabbage in two with a long blade, then tips back his head and slowly eats... the sword! There's no trick involved—sword swallowing and other sharp-edged acts such as walking on glass are genuine feats of daring, and highly dangerous for the untrained.

Dancing with scissors

In remote mountain villages of Peru, the *danza de la tijeras* (scissors dance) is half competition, half folk ritual. The traditional dancers snip at the air around them with iron rods like scissors in contests that may continue all day. In their most extreme form, the dances become flesh-tearing ordeals in which men demonstrate how much pain they can endure. In 2010 UNESCO recognized the dance as a unique part of Peru's cultural heritage.

▶ The dances may celebrate the pagan gods worshipped before the Spanish conquest of Peru in the 16th century.

Hunger pangs

Swallowing swords was once thought to be a trick, but the invention of X-ray photography showed that the blade really does go all the way down. Students of the art start by tickling their throats with small pieces of wire. This teaches them to overcome the gag reflex—the automatic tightening of the throat that normally stops us choking on food. To swallow a blade safely, they must straighten their necks so that the mouth, throat, and stomach lie in a straight line.

▶ An X-ray image of Australian stunt performer Chayne Hultgren, AKA The Space Cowboy, clearly shows the long blade he has swallowed. The Space Cowboy also swallows table legs, saws, neon lights, and hedge clippers.

Light lunch

Expert glass-chewers take care to crunch a lightbulb into very fine pieces, as swallowing bigger chunks can damage the throat and gut. Performers who specialize in eating strange objects don't stop at glass. Frenchman "Monsieur Mangetout" has eaten a bicycle, a shopping trolley, and a light aircraft.

▲ Chinese stuntman Zhang Yujian takes just 40 seconds to crunch his way through a 60-watt bulb.

SOLE SURVIVOR

Leathery feet are an advantage when it comes to walking on broken glass, but careful preparation is just as important. Performers use clean broken bottles, and move the tough, angular bases and corners to the edge of the track. A deep bed of glass ensures that it can shift underfoot, reducing the risk of sharp edges pointing upward. "Feeling the way" with the feet enables glass-walkers to shift their weight away from the sharpest pieces.

▼ At a performance in Paris, Cirque de Pekin stars put a new twist on the bed-of-nails stunt.

Sleep well

Once the speciality of Indian fakirs (Muslim holy men), lying on a bed of nails actually requires no religious faith. Though the nails are sharp, they are very closely spaced, so there is not enough pressure on a single nail to pierce the skin. However, the stunt is safe only if the performer's weight is evenly spread on the "bed." The difficult part is getting on and off—sudden movements can cause prickly problems.

Going for the RECORD

Want to pilot the fastest human-powered vehicle on land, water, or air? Then start pedaling! Spinning the cranks is the most efficient way to turn muscle power into movement, whether you're on the road, in an aircraft, or in a submarine. So between record attempts, you'll find speed heroes out training on their bikes.

Where are the brakes?

Mountain bikers relish a steep hill, but few dare to tackle slopes as steep and treacherous as those Eric Barone chooses. This French cyclist holds the world record for speedy descents on wheels. He hurtles down volcanoes and snowy peaks as fast as an express train. Specially customized bikes, including enhanced brakes, give a competitive edge.

THE INCREDIBLE SPEED AND BONE-JOLTING SHOCKS OF EXTREME DOWNHILL RIDES CAN LITERALLY SHAKE A BIKE TO PIECES.

▶ Austrian Markus Stöckl holds world records for descents on unmodified mountain bikes.

Laid-back pedaler

It's a bike, but not as we know it! Ordinary, or "diamond frame," bicycles are just too slow to break records on level courses, as their high saddle positions create air resistance that slows them down. Instead, the world's fastest bikers lie back to pedal, powering their "recumbent" bikes at more than 80 mph (130 km/h) A streamlined fairing (covering) makes the bike look—and perform—like a bullet.

▼ At 83 mph (133.5 km/h), Sam Whittingham is the fastest self-propelled person on the planet.

FASTEST
LEVEL LAND SPEED
Canadian Sam Whittingham took the world 200 m speed record for a human-powered vehicle in September 2009.

Up, up, and away

Compared to record-breaking bikes, human-powered aircraft move at a very leisurely pace. What's extraordinary is that they fly at all—they look as fragile as cobwebs. Builders shave every ounce of weight from the airframe so that the pilot's vigorous pedaling can lift himself and the 100-ft- (30-m-) wide plane just a few feet into the air. Flight alone isn't enough—to win prizes, the plane must navigate a figure-of-eight course.

FIRST
HUMAN-POWERED PLANE
Gossamer Condor completed a one-mile (1.6-km) course using nothing but pedal power.

◄ Pilot Bryan Allen is a cyclist and hang-glider enthusiast, so he was the perfect choice to pedal aircraft *Gossamer Condor* on a prize-winning flight in August 1977.

COOLEST
HUMAN-POWERED SUB
The *FAU-Boat* narrowly scooped the speed prize in 1993, beating its competitor by just 15 seconds.

Blowing bubbles

Since 1989, submarine enthusiasts have been competing to be the fastest human under water at races organized in the U.S. by the Foundation for Underwater Research and Education (FURE). Dozens of shark-shaped subs take part, each with one or two crew members turning the pedal-powered propellers. The subs are flooded with water on the 330-ft (100-m) course, and the crew breathe using SCUBA masks. The winning subs speed along at 9 mph (14 km/h) or faster.

◄ The colorful *FAU-Boat*, an entry from the Florida Atlantic University, speeds to victory at the 3rd International Submarine Races.

FASTEST
OLYMPIC SPORT
American Tony Benshoof holds the world luge speed record of 86.93 mph (139.9 km/h).

▼ Luge athletes have to cope with steep turns in the track as well as blistering speed.

Slippery slope

The fastest of all Olympic athletes don't need pedals—they rely on gravity to speed them down a hillside track glazed with ice. Luge racers lie on their backs on a sled no bigger than a tea tray. They expertly flex the sled to guide its runners. The sport of luge began in the late 19th century in the frozen streets and lanes of Swiss town St. Moritz. Today competitive races are all held on purpose-built ice tracks.

DYING
to Win

Which is more risky, jogging or skydiving? The answer may surprise you: traffic and other hazards mean you're more likely to die pounding the pavement than leaping out of a plane. Even with strict rules to promote safety, top athletes have to be super-skilled—and have a bit of luck—to stay injury-free.

Brain bangers

Strict rules, fist and face padding, and medical help make boxing safer than the bare-knuckle fistfights of the sport's origins. However, the boxing ring is still a bloody, wild place. The knockout blow to the head that wins a bout can cause permanent brain injury. Damage shows up on brain scans of four out of every five professional boxers.

▲ In this 2007 match Mexican Oscar Larios (right) took a pounding from his rival that knocked him to the floor, and lost him the contest.

▼ In matches like this international game between France and Japan, scrums are safer because the teams are equally strong. Mismatched teams are more at risk.

No protection required

Rugby players don't wear the heavy padding that protects those in NFL (National Football League) games, so you would expect them to suffer more blood, bruises, and broken bones. In fact, lack of protection makes rugby less aggressive. Scrums (when teams lock arms and heads to push and gain ground) are the most dangerous part of the game, especially when players' strength and size are unequal. If the scrum collapses, front-row players risk serious injury.

Gridiron hazards

Crrrunch! The bone-splitting sound of a tackle tells you all you need to know. The strength and aggression that's needed to succeed in American football makes it a risky game. Thanks to helmets and padding fatalities are low, but injuries remain common. Head injuries, in particular, often go unnoticed, and professional NFL players may suffer hidden brain damage that handicaps them long after their careers are over.

▶ Quentin Jammer makes a flying tackle in this match between the New England Patriots and the San Diego Chargers.

▶ Jockey W. J. Lee didn't stay long in the saddle in this 2011 race. Professional horse racing is one of the most risky sports and jockeys suffer three injuries in an average year.

Giddy up!

The dangers of being a champion jockey are obvious—high jumps and high speed can make falls fatal. But ordinary horse-riding is dangerous, too, and 120 Americans die each year in riding accidents. Horses are unpredictable and it's a long way from the saddle to the ground. So should horse-riding be banned as a dangerous sport? No! You are seven times more likely to die by choking on your food!

Jungle grotto

Some of the world's most fantastic cave systems are doubly hidden. Not only are their vast tunnel networks out of sight beneath the ground, but the entrances are buried deep in remote forests. Reaching these inaccessible caves may involve long treks through dripping jungle, carrying supplies and heavy kit. Hang Son Doong, in central Vietnam, was used as a shelter during the country's 1960s war, but locals soon forgot the cave when bombing stopped. It took cavers three expeditions just to find the entrance.

▲ Rediscovered in 2009, Son Doong (Mountain River) cave encloses a fast-flowing river, which creates an eerie whistle at the entrance. At 660 ft (200 m) in height, the biggest chamber is the largest in any cave in the world.

Into the EARTH

They are cramped, wet, cold, dangerous, and totally dark—so exactly what is the attraction of caves? The thrill of venturing into truly unexplored territory is one reason why these intrepid subterranean sportsmen spend their lives—and savings—exploring the world's deepest natural tunnels.

Muddy squeeze

Protective clothing such as boots, overalls, and a helmet are essentials for moving through low, muddy, narrow passages. One helmet light is not enough. Two provides a margin of safety, and many cavers carry a third. Even with this basic equipment, you should never start exploring caves without the help of someone who's been underground before, and never go down alone.

▲ The Krubera cave in Georgia's Caucasus Mountains burrows deeper into the earth than any other. The deepest point explorers have reached is 7,200 ft (2,200 m) below the entrance.

Rock-climbing upside down

Deep cave systems include long vertical drops that are difficult or impossible to descend or ascend using ordinary rock-climbing techniques. To tackle these obstacles, cavers must use either fold-up ladders or ascenders—devices that slide up a fixed rope, but clamp tight when pulled down. With loops of rope hung from a pair of ascenders, cavers can laboriously pull themselves up from great depths.

▲ Jagged stalactites (hanging points of rock) make the roofs of cave passages an uncomfortable obstacle. In this Thailand tunnel the caver pushes an oxygen tank ahead of her.

Deep, dark water

Flooded tunnels make a dangerous cave potentially deadly. Cavers use SCUBA equipment, but—unlike ocean divers—they cannot surface if the air runs out. There are other risks—the water can be very cold and fast-flowing, and mud can suddenly reduce visibility to zero in a "silt out." Training and specialized equipment help to reduce the risk, and cave divers tackle silt outs by letting out a guideline as they move forward. Even if mud blinds them, they can follow the line back to safety.

▲ Top cave divers endure some of the toughest environments on the planet, exploring icy cold and uncharted waters.

All at SEA

ROUTES

- - - - First solo circumnavigation (Joshua Slocum)

- - - - First nonstop circumnavigation (Chay Blyth)

- - - - Swimming the Channel (David Walliams)

- - - - Rowing the Pacific (Roz Savage)

- - - - Vendée Globe race

Sailors and swimmers who cross the world's deep waters risk drowning, exhaustion, and loneliness. So why do they do it? For many of them, it's the challenge of beating a record that drives them on. For others, it's a way of testing themselves, or achieving a long-held personal ambition.

NORTH ATLANTIC OCEAN

Boston, U.S. *Joshua Slocum start/finish*

Southampton, U.K. *Chay Blyth start/finish*

San Francisco, U.S. *Roz Savage Pacific crossing start*

PACIFIC OCEAN

Roz Savage

Hawaii

Les Sables-d'Olonne, France *Vendée Globe race start/finish*

Who started it all?

Solo voyages around the world began at the end of the 19th century with the adventures of Canadian-American seaman and boat-builder Joshua Slocum (1844–1909). In April 1895 he set sail in the *Spray*, a 37-ft (11-m) oyster boat that he had rebuilt himself. Using centuries-old navigation methods he took three years to complete the voyage.

Joshua Slocum

▶ Slocum described the huge wave that engulfed his tiny boat off South America: "She shook in every timber and reeled under the weight of the sea."

SOUTH ATLANTIC OCEAN

Chay Blyth

Round the world, the hard way

Circumnavigation (circling the world) in a sailing boat is a dangerous, difficult task. Doing it alone, and without docking at a port, is harder still. And heading westward piles on even more risk, for the boat must sail into the wind for most of the route. The first successful attempt came in 1971, when Scottish sailor Chay Blyth completed the trip in 292 days.

SOUTHERN OCEAN

Vendée Globe race

▶ Sailing in his yacht *Adrien*, French sailor Jean Luc van den Heede clipped a month from the world single-handed record for the westward round-the-world route in 2004. It took him 122 days.

Open water

To understand the challenge facing an open-water swimmer, measure their epic crossings in pool lengths. Swimming the Cook Strait between New Zealand's two islands is equivalent to 440 Olympic pool lengths. The English Channel is 675. But distance—and the tiredness and cramp it brings—is just half of the difficulty. Swimmers also brave bone-numbing cold, debris in the water, shipping, jellyfish, and sharks.

◀ British comedian David Walliams didn't break any records when he swam the English Channel in 2006, but he raised £1m ($1.5m) for charity.

Rowing the widest ocean

Most people who have rowed across an ocean haven't done so by choice—shipwreck forced them to pull on the oars or perish. Two Norwegians rowed across the Atlantic by choice in 1896, and transatlantic races began in 1997. At 7,000 mi (12,000 km) across, the Pacific is four times wider than the Atlantic. John Fairfax and Sylvia Cook were the first to cross it, from San Francisco, U.S., to Hayman Island, Australia, in 1971. They were rowing for 361 days.

▼ Roz Savage became the first woman to row across the Pacific single handed in 2010. She split her voyage into three legs, arriving in Waikiki, Hawaii (below), at the end of the first stage, one million oar strokes after leaving the Californian coast.

Roz Savage — Tarawa

PACIFIC OCEAN

Papua New Guinea
Roz Savage Pacific crossing finish

Joshua Slocum

INDIAN OCEAN

Chay Blyth

Vendée Globe race

▼ The VM Matériaux, sailed by Patrice Carpentier, crosses the starting line to begin the Vendée Globe race. A broken boom later put him out of the race.

Braving icebergs

Today, single-handed sailing around the world has become a sport. In the Vendée Globe race, solo yachtsmen and women sail from France to the Southern Ocean, race clockwise around Antarctica, and return home—all without assistance. It's a grueling, hazardous competition. High winds, monstrous waves, and sea ice force mariners to be constantly alert. None of the skippers dare sleep—instead they take short naps five or six times a day.

RISKS on Screen

Some moviegoers are becoming indifferent to special effects that they know are computer-generated, so many directors are turning back to old-fashioned stunts. Now when you see a star get shot, burned, blown up, or hurled off a building, there's a good chance that a stunt double risked their life to make the scene convincing.

Up in flames

Performing in burning clothes is one of the most dangerous of all stunts. Doubles wear several layers of fireproof clothing over their skin, then don a flesh-colored mask and gloves. Gel fuel on the costume makes the flames. Flames use up oxygen, so the double uses a mouthpiece to breathe air from a hidden cylinder. Because of the danger of the stunt, shots last only seconds before crews with fire extinguishers put out the flames.

Boom BOOM!

Exploding vehicles are too dangerous for doubles, so gasoline-filled mannequins take their place at the wheel. However, doubles may drive cars lifted by explosions. Pyrotechnics experts rig a section of a telegraph pole behind the car, with an explosive charge above it. Detonating the charge fires the pole into the ground, flipping the car.

▼ Wreathed in flames, a stuntman wrestles to remove his helmet in the stunt show *Moteurs*.

▲ Thirteen stunt doubles helped add live action realism to the 2005 German action movie *Der Clown*.

WAS THAT ME?

For a major star's stunt double, a likeness of face and physique is an advantage, but it's not absolutely essential. Makeup hides differences and directors can line up shots so that the double's face appears on screen only briefly, or not at all. Skilful cutting-in of close-ups of the real star seamlessly conceals the substitution.

▲ American actor Tom Cruise would have risked serious injury in this shot of a motorcycle wheelie, so a stunt double took his place.

Happy landings

In the early days of movie stunts, doubles who fell or jumped from heights landed on carefully stacked piles of cardboard boxes. Today, airbags break their fall. For longer drops a double will hang from a steel cable wrapped round the drum of a fan descender. As the cable unwinds, fan vanes fixed to the drum slow its spin, so that the double falls at a safe, but still convincing, speed.

◄ When Johnny Depp's double jumped from a window in *The Tourist* (2010), a canvas awning and a heap of vegetables broke his fall.

ROUGHLY FOUR STUNTMEN DIE ON FILM SETS EACH YEAR, BUT MANY MORE ARE INJURED.

▶ A career as a stuntman doesn't doesn't have to be painful and short. Greg Brazzell, who is driving this car, has made 90 films.

Hitting the asphalt

Car chases and stunts start with careful preparation of the vehicles. Mechanics strengthen the car's structure and enhance the springs and shock absorbers. They may also enhance the engine's performance. Then it's down to the driving skills of stunt doubles to put the cars where the director wants them. Stars rarely drive, even if they are experts behind the wheel, as an accident would put the whole movie at risk.

SNOW Business

For skiers who find even the most demanding routes too tame, mountaintops still have plenty to offer, though the risks are as high as the summits. Beyond the reach of the lifts, slopes wind down through obstacles such as trees and vertical cliffs, and simple mistakes can trigger a deadly fall—or an avalanche.

Board or bored?

Not long ago, skiers scorned snowboarders as inferior intruders to the slopes. Today boarding is mainstream, with resorts offering rails, half-pipes, and jumps for enthusiasts. To the hardcore boarder this "taming" of their sport is unwelcome. The most skilled are following steep skiers to higher and more vertical runs. Though some compete in races, much of the pleasure of extreme snowboarding comes from the isolation and emptiness of remote slopes.

▶ Resorts make learning snowboarding (relatively) painless. At this New Zealand ski field, novices practice flying moves with an air-mattress to protect their limbs.

Getting airborne

Leaving the snow far below is part of the thrill in all forms of extreme skiing, but in ski jumping and ski flying nothing else matters. Skiers plummet down purpose-built hills, reaching more than 60 mph (100 km/h) before taking off into the air, so landing is a critical skill. Ski flying places more emphasis on how you float through the air, though distance still matters—the world record-holder, Norwegian Johan Evensen, has soared 800 ft (250 m).

▼ To a holiday skier, the view from a ski jumping hill is terrifying. Here Johan Evensen of Norway gazes down the 400-ft (120-m) drop at Oslo's Holmenkollen Ski Arena.

Chopper me up

Lifts and graded, groomed slopes make ski holidays popular and convenient, but they also create crowds. Skiers who crave empty, unspoiled surroundings now use helicopters to escape the resorts and ski ever-higher terrain. The lower temperatures at higher altitudes ensure that the snow is deeper, and for those who can afford it, it's the ultimate skiing experience.

▶ Launching yourself into deep, white powder as the chopper powers away above your head is the ultimate ski thrill.

◀ On familiar mountains, steep skiers know every crag, and can confidently jump from cliffs like this one in Banff National Park, Canada. For visitors, though, a mountain guide is essential.

WHITE DEATH

Off-piste skiers risk dislodging deep snow on higher slopes, sending it down the mountain as an avalanche. Avalanches can bury skiers, trapping them so tightly that they cannot move or breathe. Finding avalanche victims is a slow process—ten people take an hour to search an area the size of a tennis court. Few survive beneath the snow for even half this time. To improve their chances of being found, off-piste skiers carry emergency radio beacons.

AN AVALANCHE CASCADING DOWN A MOUNTAINSIDE HAS MORE THAN HALF THE POWER OF THE ENGINES THAT LIFTED THE SPACE SHUTTLE INTO ORBIT.

Beyond black diamonds

The steepest regular trails, marked by twin black diamonds, have slopes of 45–50°. They are vertiginous enough to strike terror into the heart of even very experienced skiers. To extreme skiers, these are the warm-up slopes. The real fun begins when the slope is 60° and over. The routes they choose are all off piste—not pressed into tracks. These make extremely long, fast descents possible, with many chances to go big—perform jumps with controlled landings.

WINGS of Victory

Air racers and aerobatic teams trace their roots back over a century to the days of wire-and-canvas planes. Today's pilots fly high-performance jet and prop aircraft. Their nail-biting displays of daring, speed, and precision take them low over ground and water, or in tight-formation passes above the watching crowds.

Barnstormers and wing-walkers

When World War I ended in 1918, the U.S. government sold off hundreds of surplus aircraft. Curtis JN-4s, or "Jennies," were slower and less powerful than a small modern car. Former air force pilots began using them for barnstorming—air tricks at farming fairs. The planes' slow speed enabled pilots to perform stunts such as jumping from car to plane. Modern stunt pilots repeat Jenny performances such as wing-walking.

▲ Stunt flyers really did stand on wings for pictures, but the rackets were a pose—the slipstream would have blown the ball away.

Wingtip to wingtip

Trailing colored smoke and accompanied by earsplitting roars, an aerobatic team soars so low overhead that the airshow crowds instinctively duck. These spectacular displays are performed only by military teams because of the prohibitive cost of the jet trainers they use. Pilots are the air force elite, and must fly at least 1,500 hours before they can even apply to join the team. Only one applicant in ten is chosen. Accidents are rare, but all pilots wear parachutes for both displays and training.

1920'S FLYING TEAM 13 BLACK CATS HAD A PRICE LIST FOR STUNTS. MOST COSTLY WAS $1,500 (£960) FOR BLOWING UP THE PLANE IN MIDAIR.

▲ The Royal Air Force Red Arrows aerobatic team fly their Hawk trainers in tight formation at displays worldwide. Their support crew outnumber the nine pilots ten-to-one.

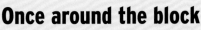

Once around the block

Racing aircraft round a circuit of pylons (tall wooden towers) began in the 1920s. At first a simple task, the difficulty and danger grew as aircraft became faster and more powerful. In modern contests, such as the Reno Air Races, pilots lap the circuits at a blistering 500 mph (800 km/h). Because of the high speeds and low altitudes at which the aircraft fly, crashes are often deadly.

▶ American pilot Michael Goulian, who is flying this Zivko Edge 540 race plane, comes from a family of pilots. He learned to fly a plane before he could drive.

International **Air Races** St Louis ~ October 1·2·3

AERONAUTICAL EXHIBITION AERO CONGRESS AIR INSTITUTE VEILED PROPHET

▲ Speeds on the graphic posters for the original air races seem quaint today, but in the 1920s, 200 mph (320 km/h) was mind-numbingly fast.

▼ Fighter aircraft like these F-16s can push pilots' bodies to the limit. As well as using g-suits, pilots tense their muscles to stay conscious.

Pulling gs

Making a tight turn forces jet pilots down into their seats, as if the force of gravity had increased, multiplying their weight. The force is measured in gs: 2 g is a doubling of gravity. High g-forces make a pilot's blood flow away from the brain, starving it of vital oxygen. At 5 or 6 g, pilots can lose consciousness. To prevent this, they wear tight g-suits with inflatable panels in the legs. In tight turns these automatically fill with air, squeezing blood back up to the brain.

Ultimate
STREET SPORTS

In organized—and televised—contests for street sports, judges give out points and prizes for skill, agility, and speed. But on the street, it's the hard, unyielding materials of the sidewalk that are the real judges. There are no second chances with concrete and tarmac, and any seasoned urban athlete has the scars to prove it.

▲ Parkour traceurs (participants) emphasize speed and efficiency, while free-runners are bigger on stunts and tricks.

LEAP OF FAITH

You can gauge how fashionable a sport has become by the number of appearances it makes in movies and commercials. By this measure, you can't get much cooler than parkour and free-running. They demand similar skills of nimbleness, fitness, judgment, and individual style. Using vaults, flips, spins, and rolls, athletes aim to move through a city with the grace of dancers.

PARKOUR'S FOUNDERS SAY THEY THINK OF THEIR SPORT AS AN ARTFORM, AND DESCRIBE THE URBAN ENVIRONMENT AS "A PLAYGROUND."

Not for safety freaks

Urban downhill mountain biking swaps steep, muddy slopes for concrete stairs. To withstand the pace, bikes have lightweight but strengthened frames with front suspension only. Competitions, such as the hair-raising Valparaiso Cerro Abajo in Chile, are run over specially constructed courses with plywood obstacles. Amateur riders can get the practice they need in sloping streets and abandoned buildings of practically any city.

◀ At the 9th Valparaiso urban downhill race in 2011 in Chile, the watching crowd get dangerously close to the speeding competitors.

Spiderman for real

Rock faces are thin on the ground in cities, but skyscrapers can be the next best thing for serious climbers. Architectural features provide hand and foot holds and anchor points—to scale New York's World Trade Center in 1977, climber George Willig fixed clamps to the window-cleaning rails. Urban climbing is sometimes called buildering—a pun on practice climbs over boulders.

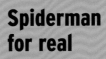

▲ Alain Robert first climbed this 32-story block in Frankfurt, Germany, in 1995. Here, 13 years on, he repeats the feat with a safety rope—and the permission of the owner, Dresdner Bank.

◀ Though it peaked in the 80s, skateboarding still has a hard core of active fans.

BIG AIR

When most people look at a city street they see curbs, walkways, rails, and benches. But through the eyes of a skateboarder the same street is a series of athletic challenges and a wealth of opportunities for stunts and tricks. Extreme streetboarding pushes this urban sport to the limit, with experts performing maneuvers that seem to defy gravity. Most escape serious injury—it's the beginners who end up kissing the concrete.

Tear up the tarmac

Street luge takes its name from the sledge on which winter sports athletes plunge down a frozen track. In street luge, though, wheels and tarmac take the place of runners and ice. Gravity causes the adapted skateboards and their riders to hurtle downhill at up to 70 mph (110 km/h)— fast enough that friction can literally melt wheels.

▲ Street luge riders wear motorcycle leathers to avoid road rash.

Cheating DEATH

To free themselves from ropes, straitjackets, chains, and prison cells, escapologists need to be fit, nimble, and skilled at picking locks and handcuffs. The traditions of their craft date back to the 18th century, but modern escapologists have added sensational twists to their acts to bring them into the age of TV and the web.

NO LOCK COULD HOLD HIM!

Harry Houdini was so famous that his name has become a word—"a Houdini" is any ingenious escape. The man behind the legend was a Hungarian-American who boasted no lock could hold him. In a career lasting 35 years he escaped from chains, boxes, mailbags, graves, and water-filled tanks, as well ropes and handcuffs. Houdini also claimed he could take a blow from anyone's fist, but in 1926 a student punched him before he could prepare himself and he died from an infection the next day.

EUROPE'S ECLIPSING SENSATION

HOUDINI

THE WORLD'S HANDCUFF KING & PRISON BREAKER

"NOTHING ON EARTH CAN HOLD HOUDINI A PRISONER"

BIG FREEZE!

DEEP DANGER!

DO OR DIE

Modern escapologists have to do much more than just escape—they need to be all-round entertainers. Houdini's audiences were content to watch a curtain for half an hour while he escaped behind it, but today this would seem ridiculous. Escape artists now perform in full view, and usually also add another attraction to their act, such as magic. Some of them, such as Thomas Solomon, deliberately avoid Houdini's escapes, while others perform them with new, dangerous features. They don't reveal their secrets, though Solomon admits to using the magician's old trick of misdirection—he distracts his audience at a crucial moment, so that they overlook the move that frees him.

DAVID MERLINI

Equipped with hammers and blowtorches, David Merlini's crew free him from the block of ice in which he has been frozen for 33 hours. This 2001 stunt is among the most spectacular that the Hungarian escapologist has performed.

DAVID BLAINE

Endlessly inventive, American David Blaine is one of the world's most high-profile escape artists. In 2006, he was chained to a gyroscope near Times Square in New York, U.S. He freed himself after two days and nights of spinning.

SPIN CYCLE

DIY ESCAPES

Escapes from handcuffs and ropes are the easiest to perform. Handcuffs are kept tight around the wrists by a simple click-latch. To open the latch, escapologists just slide in a shim—a sliver of metal small enough to hide under the tongue. Knots are almost as easy—during the knotting, deep breaths and muscle tension expand the escapologist's body. After relaxing and breathing out, they can wriggle free.

CONSENTINO

Australian escape artist "Consentino" is a self-taught illusionist. His 2010 escape from chains and handcuffs in Melbourne's shark-infested aquarium was a tribute to Houdini's plunge from the city's Queens Bridge a century earlier.

FLAMING DARE!

DEAN GUNNARSON

Harry Houdini invented the hanging straitjacket escape, but modern escapologists like Dean Gunnarson take it to another level. In this performance in Melbourne, Australia, the rope burns as he struggles to free himself from chains high above the ground.

Survival
OF THE FITTEST

The world is running out of truly unexplored places—an airliner can fly to anywhere on the globe within 24 hours. But this doesn't spell the end of adventure, or risk. Ice, rock, ocean, and jungle wilderness still beckon the brave, and the stories of their ordeals and narrow escapes inspire those of us who dare not follow them.

MOUNTAIN ODYSSEY

Your buddy hangs from a safety rope. If you cut it, you might live. If you don't, you'll both die. What would you do?

The climb, and the agonizing decision that Simon Yates took, were turned into the gripping 1983 movie *Touching the Void*.

This was the awful choice facing Simon Yates in the Peruvian Andes in 1985. He and Joe Simpson were climbing the 20,813-ft (6,344-m) Siula Grande. They reached the summit, and were on the descent when Joe slipped and broke his leg.

Simon began lowering Joe on two knotted ropes, but the injured climber went over a cliff. The two could not see or hear each other. There was no way Simon could save his buddy, so he made the dreadful decision to cut the rope. Simon spent another night on the mountain before descending to their base camp. Feeling fearful and guilty, he looked for his climbing partner but there was no sign of him. Simon decided that Joe must have died in the fall. But Joe had survived. When the rope went slack he plunged into a crevasse, dug a snow cave, and fell asleep. When he awoke, he began an epic three-day journey, without food and with very little water. Nursing his injured leg, he crawled and hopped the 5 mi (8 km) back to base camp, arriving just hours before Simon planned to pack up the camp and leave.

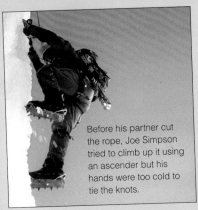

Before his partner cut the rope, Joe Simpson tried to climb up it using an ascender but his hands were too cold to tie the knots.

Struck down in the Pacific

For a couple of seasoned sailors like Richard Sharp and his fiancée Tami Oldham, it sounded like the dream job: a four-week cruise from Tahiti, delivering a luxury yacht to San Diego. But a hurricane turned the dream into a nightmare.

They knew it was going to be a big storm—the weather reports told them that. But Richard and Tami were completely unprepared for what Hurricane Raymond hurled at their sails that October day in 1983. Tami was below checking the barometer when a wave literally plucked the storm-battered yacht from the water… and dropped it from the height of a five-story building. It was more than a day before Tami recovered consciousness. The sea was calm. The sky was blue. But Richard was gone. So were the mast and the radio. When she had recovered from the shock, Tami rigged a tiny sail from the wreckage, and turned the boat toward the nearest downwind island. For Tami, there was no rescue boat, and no spotter plane. She sailed her crippled craft 1,500 mi (2,400 km) all the way to Hilo Harbor, Hawaii.

"I CHECKED THE WIND-SPEED GAUGE AND GASPED WHEN I READ 140 KNOTS."

Two weeks in an ice cave

In 1982 Mark Inglis and Phil Doole were near the top of New Zealand's Mount Cook when a blizzard hit. They were experienced climbers, so they dug a snow cave, climbed in, and waited for the storm to subside.

But the storm didn't let up. Outside what they called their "hotel," 90-mph (145-km/h) winds howled. Inside, the temperature fell to -4°F (-20°C). Over the next five days they shared five biscuits—the only food they had. Their legs turned numb, then froze to ice. On the seventh day, a helicopter dropped supplies. Six days later, they were rescued. It was too late to save their frozen legs, which were amputated (cut off) above the knee. Amazingly this terrible ordeal did not quell their enthusiasm for climbing— Mark went on to climb Everest, becoming the first double-amputee to do so.

Mark Inglis worked with an artificial limb maker to create a range of legs for amputee athletes.

Surviving a traumatic climbing experience didn't put double-amputee Mark Inglis off conquering Everest. Here he shows the media his frostbitten fingers upon his return from Kathmandu.

Mega mountain

At 12,316 ft (3,754 m) high, Mount Cook is New Zealand's highest peak. Mark Inglis finally reached the summit 20 years after his ordeal.

Danger close to home

Aron on the set of *127 Hours*, the 2010 feature film of his accident.

Ours is a crowded, tamed world. Yet, as one hiker found, there is always adventure—and danger—close to home.

Hiking alone in 2003 in Utah, U.S., Aron Ralston moved a boulder. It pinned his right arm to the side of the canyon. After four days, he realized his only chance of escape was to cut off his arm with his blunt pocket-knife. He did it, climbed from the canyon, and was taken to safety by passing tourists.

Lost in the jungle

"I was obsessed with the idea of exploration" says Israeli backpacker Yossi Ghinsberg. But his lust for travel—and gold—almost cost him his life in the tangled rain forest of Bolivia.

Yossi was traveling in South America with two friends when a shady Australian told them of the remote Tuichi River, where gold glitters among the pebbles. The four men set off to find it, but after weeks of jungle trekking, they doubted their guide's skills, and split up. Yossi and an American friend boarded a raft, aiming to float downriver. The river turned to rapids, and the raft to wreckage. Yossi was washed up on a beach, alone. For three weeks he braved sickness, hunger, quicksand, leeches, and jaguars, and had almost given up hope when his friend returned in a motorboat—and ferried him to safety.

Yossi Ghinsberg's guide promised to take them to an unmapped part of the Tuichi River, where the local people guarded "huge chunks of gold" that would make them rich.

INDEX